Exploring Our Oceans

HAMMERHEAD
SHARKS

SAMANTHA BELL

Published in the United States of America by Cherry Lake Publishing
Ann Arbor, Michigan
www.cherrylakepublishing.com

Consultants: Dominique A. Didier, PhD, Associate Professor, Department of Biology, Millersville University; Marla Conn, ReadAbility, Inc.
Editorial direction: Red Line Editorial
Book design and illustration: Sleeping Bear Press

Photo Credits: iStockphoto/Thinkstock, cover, 1, 11, 17, 22, 29; Mark Doherty/Shutterstock Images, 5, 19; Sleeping Bear Press, 7; Brandelet/Shutterstock Images, 9; Dorling Kindersley RF/Thinkstock, 13; PRNewsFoto/Mandalay Bay/AP Images, 15; Ethan Daniels/Shutterstock Images, 21; Valerio D'Ambrogi/ Shutterstock Images, 25; Vincent Yu/AP Images, 27

Library of Congress Cataloging-in-Publication Data
Bell, Samantha.
  Hammerhead sharks / Samantha Bell.
    p. cm. — (Exploring our oceans)
  Audience: 008.
  Audience: Grades 4 to 6.
  Includes index.
  ISBN 978-1-62431-408-7 (hardcover) — ISBN 978-1-62431-484-1 (pbk.) — ISBN 978-1-62431-446-9 (pdf)
  — ISBN 978-1-62431-522-0 (ebook)
  1. Hammerhead sharks—Juvenile literature. I. Title.

QL638.95.S7B45 2014
597.3'4—dc23   2013006182

Cherry Lake Publishing would like to acknowledge the work of
The Partnership for 21st Century Skills. Please visit www.p21.org
for more information.

Printed in the United States of America
Corporate Graphics Inc.
July 2013
CLFA11

ABOUT THE AUTHOR

Samantha Bell is a children's book writer, illustrator, teacher, and mom of four busy kids. Her articles, short stories, and poems have been published online and in print. She loves the outdoors, nature, and animals, but she will not be going into the ocean at dusk anymore.

TABLE OF CONTENTS

CHAPTER 1

UNUSUAL SHARKS

Many strange and amazing creatures call the ocean home. With a wide, flat head and round eyes on each side, the hammerhead shark can be counted as one of the strangest. Its unusual shape may help it swim better, see farther, and find food more quickly.

There are nine species of hammerhead sharks, though more species may still be undiscovered. Most are named for the shape of their heads. The winghead has a head shaped like airplane wings. The bonnethead, also known as the shovelhead, has a head like a round shovel. Other

A hammerhead shark is easily recognized by its head shape.

LOOK AGAIN

DOES THE HAMMERHEAD LOOK DIFFERENT FROM OTHER SHARKS YOU KNOW? HOW SO? WHAT FEATURES ARE DIFFERENT FROM OTHER SHARKS YOU THINK OF?

species include the scoophead, the scalloped hammerhead, the mallethead, and the smooth hammerhead. Some hammerheads are named for other features. The great hammerhead is the largest of the hammerhead sharks. The smalleye hammerhead has the smallest eyes.

People don't have to dive too deep in the ocean to find these unusual fish. Most hammerheads prefer to swim in shallow waters close to shore. They can also be seen around **continental shelves** and coral reefs. Some are deeper swimmers, however, swimming as far as 1,000 feet (305 m) below the surface.

As tropical sharks, hammerheads prefer warmer water, and different species can be found all over the world. There are hammerheads in the Atlantic Ocean, the Pacific Ocean, the Indian Ocean, and the Red Sea. They can be found from North Carolina to Uruguay, from Great Britain to South Africa, and from Japan to Australia.

RANGE MAP

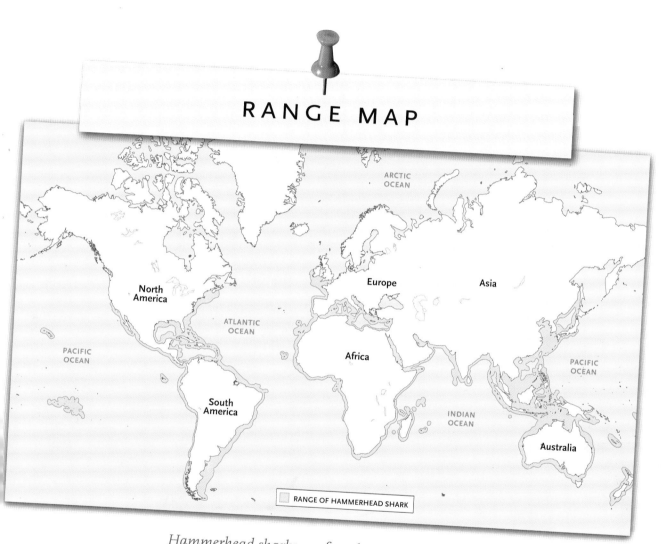

PACIFIC OCEAN

ARCTIC OCEAN

North America

ATLANTIC OCEAN

Europe

Asia

Africa

PACIFIC OCEAN

South America

INDIAN OCEAN

Australia

☐ RANGE OF HAMMERHEAD SHARK

Hammerhead sharks are found mostly along coasts.

Hammerheads sometimes travel long distances in a single day. Some will **migrate** as the seasons change, moving closer to the equator during the winter and away from it in the summer. Though many hammerheads swim alone, certain species will also move in schools. Schools of scalloped hammerheads can have hundreds of sharks, all swimming and turning in the same direction at the same time. Bonnetheads swim in smaller groups of about 15 sharks. During migration times, they travel in groups of hundreds or even thousands.

Most hammerheads are not **aggressive**. Only the three largest species have been known to attack people. They are the great hammerheads, the scalloped hammerheads, and the smooth hammerheads. Many of the smaller hammerheads, such as the winghead, have been considered mostly harmless to humans. Like all sharks, though, even these hammerheads are predators and should be treated with respect.

A school of hammerhead sharks swims in the Pacific Ocean.

CHAPTER 2

UNIQUE HEADS

The hammerhead shark is one of the easiest sharks to recognize. Its head looks like a hammer or a shovel from above. The winghead has the widest head. It can grow to about 2.5 feet (0.8 m) wide.

On each end of the head is a round eye. Each eye has a **retractable** eyelid that comes up from the bottom of the eye. This eyelid is thick and tough. When the shark is hunting or in trouble, the eyelids cover its eyes completely. These retractable eyelids protect the shark's eyes from getting hurt.

The hammerhead shark has a small mouth compared to the size of its head.

LOOK AGAIN

LOOK CLOSELY AT THE HAMMERHEAD IN THIS PHOTOGRAPH. IN WHAT WAYS DO YOU THINK ITS HEAD SHAPE HELPS THE SHARK?

Like all sharks, hammerheads have good night vision. But hammerheads have an advantage other sharks do not because of the unique shape of their heads. They can see nearly everything around them. They can even see far behind them when they move their heads back and forth.

The biggest part of a shark's brain is the part that controls its sense of smell. That means sharks can smell prey a long way off—as far as .25 mile (0.4 km) away. Once a shark smells its prey, it follows that scent through the water. The shark zigzags through the water and turns its head from side to side. That way, it can smell the odor with one nostril at a time. The shark will go in the direction of the nostril that detects a stronger smell. The hammerhead has an advantage here too. Its nostrils are far apart on its head. This makes it easier to find the right direction to swim.

Sharks do not breathe through their nostrils though. Sharks breathe by using their gills to get oxygen from the water. All sharks, including hammerheads, must have water pass over their gills in order to breathe. Because of this, hammerheads are almost always swimming.

Like all sharks, the hammerhead has no bones. Its skeleton is made up of **cartilage**. Cartilage is more flexible than bone, but it is still strong enough to give protection and support. Because it is lightweight, cartilage helps the shark stay off the bottom of the ocean. Sharks also have large livers filled with oil that help them float. Some scientists think hammerheads use their strangely shaped heads to give them extra lift.

BODY DIAGRAM

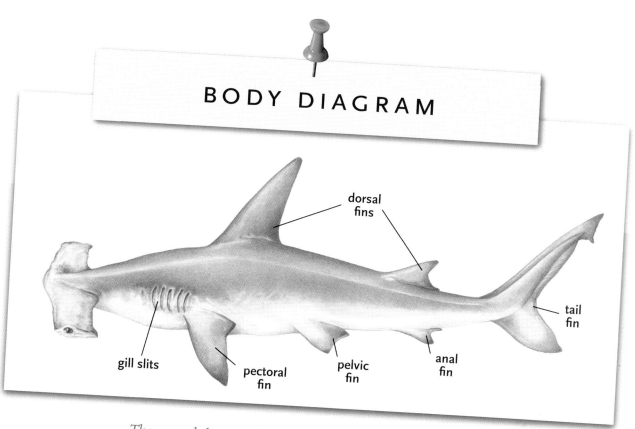

dorsal
fins

tail
fin

gill slits

pectoral
fin

pelvic
fin

anal
fin

The smooth hammerhead grows to about 8 feet (2.4 m) long.

Almost all hammerheads are gray or brown on top with white or a lighter color underneath. Most are small and don't grow longer than 5 feet (1.5 m). Just three species—the great hammerhead, the scalloped hammerhead, and the smooth hammerhead—grow a bit longer than that. The largest great hammerhead reported was 20 feet (6.1 m) long. ◢

— CHAPTER 3 —

HUNTING AND EATING

Hammerheads hunt at dawn and dusk. Like other sharks, they are **carnivores**. Some believe the hammerhead's strange shape helps it catch prey. If the prey changes direction quickly and shoots away, the shark's "hammer" helps it turn around fast and catch the prey.

Bonnetheads prefer fish, snails, shrimp, and crabs. They have small, sharp teeth in the front for grabbing their prey and flat teeth in back to break the hard shells. Smooth hammerheads eat bony fish, stingrays, skates, and small sharks. Scalloped and smooth hammerheads feed on squid.

Hammerhead sharks have smaller teeth than many other sharks.

Great hammerheads eat fish such as grouper, catfish, and flatfish, but they add a little danger to their menu. They also eat poisonous fish, which do not harm the sharks. The puffer fish and trunkfish are two of their favorites. Great hammerheads love to eat stingrays, even though they are poisonous too.

Sharks have an amazing way to "hear" their prey. They have special organs called lateral lines that run from their heads to their tails. The lateral-line system helps a shark feel vibrations in the water using its whole body. The lateral lines are on both sides of the shark, just under its skin. They have tiny sensory cells inside them. These cells tell the shark whenever there is any movement in the water. Hammerheads use their lateral-line systems when hunting. They can detect nearly every movement in the water within 300 feet (91 m).

Hammerhead sharks have another way of finding food. All living things create electrical signals. These signals don't travel through air or land, but they move well in water, especially salt water. Sharks have tiny holes on their snouts and heads that work like **receptors**. These receptors pick up the electrical signals. A shark can detect its prey's electrical signals even if the animal is resting under the sand.

The hammerhead has receptors all across the bottom of its flat head. As it hunts, the shark sweeps its head over the ocean floor like a metal detector. It finds the stingrays and flatfish hidden under the sand. Because its head is so wide, it can cover a big area with one sweep.

GO DEEPER

READ THE PREVIOUS THREE PARAGRAPHS CLOSELY. COMPARE A HUMAN'S FIVE SENSES TO THE SENSORY ORGANS OF A SHARK. WHY DO YOU THINK THEY ARE SO DIFFERENT?

When a great hammerhead finds a stingray under the sand, it uses its head to hold the stingray to the ground. Then it twists around and bites part of the stingray's wing so it can't move. The great hammerhead then feeds on the animal.

A hammerhead shark swims in a school of fish to catch its prey.

CHAPTER 4

PUPS AND GROWING UP

When you hear about a litter of **pups**, you probably think of baby dogs. But baby hammerhead sharks are called pups too. The number of pups a hammerhead has depends on its species. The bonnethead has from four to 16 pups. The smooth hammerhead has 20 to 40 pups. A great hammerhead has about six to 42 pups.

Hammerhead sharks don't lay eggs. Instead, the babies grow inside the mother. Female bonnetheads give birth after four or five months. This is the shortest amount of

Mother hammerheads travel to nurseries to
give birth to their young in safe places.

time for any shark. Most female hammerheads are pregnant for almost a year.

In the early months, the **embryos** use a yolk sac for food. Later, the embryos receive nourishment and oxygen directly from the mother's bloodstream. In the spring, summer, or early fall, the mother will give birth to live babies.

When a scalloped hammerhead is ready to give birth, she will find a shallow area to have her pups. This shallow area is called a nursery. In this nursery, there are few predators, and the pups will find plenty to eat.

The pups look a lot like their parents, but the pups' heads are a bit rounder. They have a full set of teeth, and they are soon searching for something to eat. The size of the new pups depends on the species. Smalleye hammerhead pups are about 12 inches (30.5 cm) long. Smooth hammerheads measure about 20 inches (50.8 cm) long. Great hammerhead pups can measure more than 2 feet (70 cm) long.

Hammerhead shark pups look very similar to adults.

Hammerheads swim together until they are mature.

LOOK AGAIN

LOOK AT THE HAMMERHEADS IN THIS PHOTOGRAPH. WHY DO YOU THINK PUPS ARE BORN LOOKING SO MUCH LIKE THE ADULTS AND WITH FULL SETS OF TEETH?

Pups stay in the safe nursery for different periods of time. Some leave the nursery when they are three or four months old. Others may stay for a couple years. When they leave, the young hammerheads will often swim together in large schools for years until they mature.

It is a while still before the sharks are old enough to have pups of their own. Female hammerheads take about ten to 15 years to mature. Males are not mature until they are about six to ten years old. Hammerheads can live to be about 20 to 30 years old. ◢

— CHAPTER 5 —

THREATS

Hammerhead sharks are **apex** predators. They have few natural enemies in the ocean. Pups, smaller hammerheads, and injured hammerheads may become prey to larger sharks.

But there are manmade dangers facing hammerhead sharks. Some of the biggest threats to hammerheads come from **fisheries**. Some fisheries set out nets and lines for other fish. The hammerheads get caught in these nets and die. Scalloped hammerheads are often caught accidentally with other large fish such as tuna.

Hammerhead sharks can get caught in nets meant for other fish.

Some fisheries try to catch the sharks. Shark meat isn't expensive but the fins are. Many times, the sharks are caught and only their fins are taken. People pay a lot of money for the shark fins to make shark fin soup. It is a special dish in several Asian countries. People want to serve the soup at weddings, birthdays, and important business meetings. The soup is also becoming more common in restaurants. It is very expensive. One bowl of soup can cost $100 or more. Because so many people want it and it is so expensive, fishermen can earn a lot of money selling the fins. The hammerhead's fins are some of the most valuable for this soup.

Some species of sharks are in danger at all ages. Some fisheries catch scalloped hammerhead pups and juveniles near the shore. Others go after large schools to get a bigger catch. Fishermen travel all over the globe to find them and take their fins. In fact, so many scalloped hammerheads have been caught that they, and the great hammerhead, are in danger of becoming **extinct**.

Hammerhead shark fins are sold at high prices for shark fin soup.

Fortunately, the United States banned shark finning in 1993. Now it is illegal to take only the shark fins in the U.S. Atlantic and the Gulf of Mexico. The sharks in the Pacific are mostly unprotected. Also, sharks migrate to other areas. Even if they are protected in the Atlantic, they are in danger when they swim to other waters.

Tourism is another threat to hammerheads. Many coastal areas where hammerheads live are being developed for tourists. Hotels and pollution are affecting the nurseries where pups are born and grow. This means hammerheads have fewer safe places to give birth.

THINK ABOUT IT
WHAT OTHER STEPS COULD BE TAKEN TO PROTECT THE HAMMERHEAD SHARKS OF THE WORLD?

Like other sharks, hammerheads breed slowly. The sharks take years to mature, and they have pups only every other year. Because of this, it is important their nurseries remain so they can give birth in safe places.

Groups around the world are working to make sure hammerhead populations don't get too small. Researchers are looking for better ways to protect them. They hope hammerheads will be around for a long time. ◢

Researchers continue to study hammerhead sharks to try to find better ways to protect them.

THINK ABOUT IT

▲ Many hammerheads are named for the shape of their heads. If there were a spoonhead, what might it look like? Describe its key features.

▲ Some people are afraid of sharks. Others find them fascinating. What did you think about sharks before reading this book? After reading about hammerheads, what do you think about sharks now?

▲ Read Chapter 4 again. What do you think is one of its main ideas? Provide two reasons why you think this.

▲ Some species of hammerheads are in danger of becoming extinct. What do you think people can do to stop this from happening?

LEARN MORE

BOOKS

Marsico, Katie. *Sharks*. New York: Scholastic, 2011.

Musgrave, Ruth. *Everything Sharks*. Washington, DC: National Geographic, 2011.

Smith, Miranda. *Sharks*. New York: Kingfisher, 2008.

WEB SITES

National Geographic—Sharks
http://animals.nationalgeographic.com/animals/sharks

Readers discover different species of sharks, learn more about the ocean, and play games at this Web site.

Shark Trust
http://www.sharktrust.org/juniors

On this Web site, readers can watch shark videos, play games, learn fun facts, and even adopt a shark.

GLOSSARY

aggressive (uh-GREH-siv) showing violent behavior

apex (AY-pex) at the very top

carnivore (KAR-nuh-vor) an animal that eats meat

cartilage (KAHR-tuh-lij) a hard, flexible tissue that forms certain parts of animals' bodies, such as a human ear or a shark's skeleton

continental shelf (kahn-tuh-NEN-tuhl SHELF) the part of the sea floor that slopes into the water before a steep drop to the ocean floor

embryo (EM-bree-oh) a baby that has not yet developed much

extinct (ik-STINGKT) no longer found alive

fishery (FISH-ur-ee) the industry of catching, processing, and selling fish

migrate (MYE-grate) to move from one area to another

pup (PUP) a baby shark

receptor (ri-SEHP-tur) a group of cells that receives something, like electrical signals

retractable (ri-TRAK-tuh-bul) able to be pulled back in

INDEX

[21ST CENTURY SKILLS LIBRARY]